D0184413

HUMPHREY

The Nine Lives of the Number Ten Cat

HUMPHREY

The Nine Lives of the Number Ten Cat

Willie Rushton

PAVILION

AUTHOR'S NOTE

— ◆ —

In each picture of a Prime Minister
are a number of mice –
you may like to look for them.
Why not? 'Something for
all the family' is my motto.

First published in Great Britain in 1995 by
PAVILION BOOKS LIMITED
26 Upper Ground, London SE1 9PD

Designed by Bet Ayer

A CIP catalogue record for this book is available
from the British Library.

ISBN 1 85793 806 2

Set in Leawood Book
Printed in Spain by Bookprint

2 4 6 8 10 9 7 5 3 1

This book can be ordered direct from the publisher. Please contact
the Marketing Department. But try your bookshop first

I, Garpington Thunderstorm Auberon Buchanan Borchester
Garth Chesterton Gustavus Adolphus 'Schnozzle' Cat was born
seven or eight lives ago at Snoring Hall, Wiltshire, home of
Lord and Lady Snoring-Snoring, the famous collectors and
explorers.

('How do you spell Garpthing?' asks Old Ginger of the
Catlittery Review, to whom I am dictating My Life.

'I don't,' I reply. 'For the last life or two I have been known
to my masters as Humphrey, after some television programme
that Mrs Thatcher liked. A name I hate, quite frankly, and which
I can't spell either.')

Lord Snoring-Snoring was internationally renowned for his
collection of manhole covers, the largest in the world.

One morning when I was very young, I was having breakfast with Lord and Lady Snoring-Snoring. About once a year they invited one of us cats from the Stable Block up to the Hall. It was usually a reward for something. I may well have been Mouser of the Year.

('Mouser of the Year?' repeats Old Ginger, gingerly picking out the letters on his ancient typewriter, and clearly impressed.

'I was a Tiger in my youth,' I reply.)

So there I sat nervously eating my kipper. To this day I'm not sure where you're meant to spit the bones. Suddenly, a large green bird landed on Lord Snoring-Snoring's head. I think it came from Paraguay.

('A long flight at that time of day,' Old Ginger interrupts my flow.

'It came *originally* from Paraguay,' I say rather irritably, 'not at that precise moment. Lord Snoring-Snoring brought the bird back from one of his expeditions.')

Lord Snoring-Snoring appeared not to notice the large green bird on his head, and carried on reading his newspaper. Then we all jumped as he looked up, glared down the table at Lady Snoring-Snoring, and shouted, 'Why are you staring at me like that? Stare, stare, stare! WHY?'

'A cat', she said, bowing slightly in my direction, 'may look at a Queen.'

I don't know why she said it, but it was the first time I'd heard about it. Mother had told me several times that a cat had Nine Lives, but not this.

A cat may look at a Queen, eh? And feeling young and immortal, this new piece of information seemed much more important than the stuff about Nine Lives, which at the time sounded like an unnecessary luxury.

The Snoring-Snorings were still staring at each other through an atmosphere you could cut into slices and sell as hassocks, so I slipped away to see Mother.

She was in her usual spot in the Stable Block. She'd spent the morning thoroughly enjoying herself, driving the foxhounds mad in their kennels round the back. Serve them right. You'd never find cats behaving like that. Certainly not in packs. Just to make humans feel superior.

'Mother,' I said sternly and rather pompously, 'you never told me that a cat may look at a Queen.' I must admit that at that moment I had no idea what a Queen was or why one would be interested in a viewing.

'I was saving it up until you were older,' she replied.

'What is a Queen, then?' I asked.

'It's a sort of human equivalent of me,' she said. 'It's the head of a tribe or pack or whatever.' And she surveyed her patch in a haughty manner and I knew exactly what she meant. Even the horses were wary of her.

'Where can I look at one?' I asked, in a casual sort of manner.

'There aren't many left,' said Mother, 'but there's one in London.'

———— ◆ ————

Getting to London was not going to be a major problem. I've told you that the Snoring-Snorings were famous explorers, and so almost every week a van or vans would come down from the Army and Navy Stores in London, full of tents and flags, canvas baths and buckets, tins of pemmican and figs, and crates of gin and Worcester Sauce.

'The Army and Navy Stores', said Mother, 'are very near Buckingham Palace where the Queen lives.'

I woke up when the van stopped with a screech of brakes, a sound not unlike the large, green bird. There was a lot of noise and smoke, odd smells and strange music. This must be London, I thought.

I found Buckingham Palace easily enough. Crossing the road was another matter, but I hid among the feet of a party of tourists, closed my eyes and there I was. The gates looked massive, and I had hardly stepped inside them, before I was surrounded.

'And where do we think we are going?' smirked a guardsman. He was being cute. Too much Christopher Robin, in my view.

'Lost, are we, sonny boy? Lost our Mummy, have we?' Now a Yeoman of the Guard was getting up my nose. Health Warning: Never Patronise a Cat. I could hardly wait for the Household Cavalryman's contribution.

'Shall I cut his head off with my sword?' he laughed.

'Steady the Buffs!' said a policeman. 'We shall alarm the tiny creature. I'll take him round to the kitchens.' This was excellent news. I hadn't eaten since breakfast. '*She'll* give him a bit of fish and the like.'

SHE!!! I've not been in London an hour and already I am on the brink of taking fish with the Queen. I had no idea cats carried such clout in the Big City. The policeman, towards whom I had warmed, picked me up.

'Who's an itsy-bitsy, goo-goo, ickle pussy-wussy, then?' *This* from a policeman to whom I had warmed.

We all marched round to the back of the Palace. Well, the humans all marched. I was carried. I could smell baking.

The policeman dropped me at an open door. 'In you go, little fellow,' he said. 'Introduce yourself. She's very fond of animals.'

I came as a bit of a shock to Her Majesty. Though she was everything I had imagined, and more. She was in the middle of icing a cake when I miaowed loudly and bowed.

'Oo! Ello!' she said when she had recovered. 'Who are you, then? Like a cup of tea?' She seemed not to know that milk is our tipple. I thought perhaps she was more of a dog person.

('There are those', said Old Ginger sadly, 'who prefer . . .' He couldn't say 'Dogs'. He simply shook his head. Perhaps he's not all bad, after all.)

The Queen looked at the name-tag on my collar. 'Cat?' she said. 'Cat? That's a boring name.'

I couldn't explain to her that it wasn't my name. It was to remind Lord Snoring-Snoring what I was. He could remember names but not species. The horses had labels saying 'Horse' on them. The camels had labels saying 'Camel'. Lady Snoring-Snoring had a brooch saying 'Wife'.

I took tea with Her Majesty. Some delicious sardines. 'By Appointment' it said on the tin. 'Purveyors of Delicious Sardines to H.M. The Queen.' She let me lick the icing off a small cake.

'So,' she said after tea, 'you're lost, homeless and out of work. Well, I have an idea. They're looking for a mouser at Number Ten.' I had no idea what she was talking about.

('Number Ten is where the Prime Minister lives,' said Old Ginger, who is a know-all. 'Number Ten, Downing Street.'

'Every Prime Minister since Sir Robert Walpole in 1732 has lived there,' I riposted quickly, 'though I imagine that that is a fact that any sensible Estate Agent will gloss over when it comes to the inevitable selling-off. And I have worked under the last nine.')

The first Prime Minister that I worked under was Sir Winston Churchill. He was a Great Man. And when I first met him, he was a Grand Old Man. He had done tremendous things in several Wars that humans are always having. They all said he was terrifically good at War, but didn't know what to do with himself in Peace. Humans are very violent. That is why we cats sit on them.

(I didn't know that,' says old Ginger.

'It's to stop them getting up and hitting each other. It is also a well-known fact that stroking a cat is very good for humans. It calms them down.'

'Well, I never,' says Old Ginger.)

Sir Winston had an ample lap and enjoyed rubbing my ears. Sometimes when he was painting, which he used to do when waiting for the next war, that and brick laying, he would use me as a rag.

He had trouble saying 'esses' and they sounded like 'eshes'. I used to sit outside the bathroom door listening to him shaving and practising his Oratory, for which he was also famous. 'Shlurp! Shlurp!' he would go. 'NEVAH! Shlurp! Gargle! Gargle! Nevah! Show many! Show few! Show much! Shlurp!'

It was this speech defect that caused the loss of my first life. He said 'Hello, puss!' to me and I thought he said 'Hello, push!' so I gave him a friendly shove behind the knees, and over he went and I was nearly cut in half by a falling bookshelf full of books. *His* books. He also wrote a lot. When I came round, he'd resigned. I think it was the shock.

Churchill said, 'There'sh thish one moush that I want you to find. Hish name ish Adolf.' I can't see him, I must be going blind.

The next Prime Minister was a totally different bottle of fish. Sir Anthony Eden. Mister Immaculate, I called him. He reminded me of Fred Astaire, the wonderful dancer. He was tall and lean and elegant with a neat moustache, and he had a hat named after him. I think I envied him that most. Sir Winston had many things named after him: a College at Cambridge, a tank, a theatre, lots of streets and a large number of public houses, but never a hat.

Mr Eden had a thing about dictators. He'd had a lot of trouble with Adolf Hitler and Mussolini.

('He wasn't the only one!' says Old Ginger, who is old enough to remember the War, and never lets you forget it.)

Suddenly another dictator enters his life. Colonel Nasser who blocked the Sewage Canal, or that's what I thought he said. It was hard to understand anything he said. He was raving on about the Egyptians, and how they'd got right up his nose, and he was sending the Army, the Navy and the Air Force to give them what-for. Well, as a cat I won't hear a word against the Egyptians. They used to worship us as gods, which is even better than having a hat named after you. I will admit I have in my time had a good deal of trouble with Persians and Siamese and Burmese, not to mention fat Ginger Toms.

('Thank you very much,' says Old Ginger, making a point of not writing down the last bit.)

Even so I have never wished bombs upon them, which is just as well as Sir Anthony wished bombs upon the Egyptians and nobody liked him at all after that. I never spoke to him again. Or danced with him. He resigned almost immediately.

'There are two mice here,' said Eden, 'an unattractive pair.
Sometimes behind the curtain. Sometimes upon the stair.'

My favourite Prime Minister came next – Mr Harold Macmillan. Everyone seemed to like him. Probably because everything else in Britain at that time was going faster and faster and swinging and jumping and bopping and changing. Mr Macmillan did none of these things. In the middle of all the excitement and noise he appeared wonderfully old-fashioned and peaceful. He wore baggy tweeds and cardigans and a very old shaggy moustache. When he went to Moscow he wore a large white fur hat that put the Russian ones to shame. He gave it to me later to sleep on. It only fell to bits quite recently.

He didn't actually say 'You never had it so good' but he said something quite like it, and everybody seemed to agree. All humans want are televisions and washing machines, and under Mr Macmillan they all seemed to have them. This obviously made him very popular.

He only had one fault, and it led to my best job at Number Ten. After dinner, when the port and cigars had been handed round, he would stand in front of the mantelpiece and hold forth for several hours, lecturing his guests on the Peloplenesian Wars.

('What!?' says Old Ginger, 'come again.'

'That was when the Romans sacked Carthage, and Hannibal crossed the Alps with a lot of elephants,' I explained.)

My job, for which I was handsomely rewarded, was to keep his guests awake. This I did by jumping on their faces.

'Nobody goes to sleep while I'm on,' said Harold. He sometimes behaved like an old actor. We were all sorry to see him go.

'In this room,' said Macmillan, 'I'd say there were three,
A formidable trio of mice.'
'Righty ho, sir!' I lied, for I couldn't see one,
'I'll be dealing with them in a trice.'

My friend Harold was followed by Lord Home, who had to give up being Lord Home to be Prime Minister, and became Sir Alec Douglas-Home, when he could have been Mister Home. If I was a human I'd be a Mister. They seem to be a much nicer class of person. One of the other problems was how to pronounce 'Home'. I wrote a little verse:

> Lord Home, pronounced 'Home' as in 'Rome',
> No, that's wrong, Home must rhyme with 'assume'.
> When he entered a room,
> Some cried 'Hum!', he said 'Whom?'

(Cats can't write the fifth line of limericks. Sad but true.)

Everyone agreed that Sir Alec was an awfully nice chap. He had no idea about Economics, and confessed publicly that he could only work things out by counting matches. This is a great improvement on most of the politicians I have met. Not that Sir Alec ever struck me as a politician. He was a Scots Laird and seemed to miss the Grummocks and the Trussocks and the Bottocks of his native heath. He was never happier than when he took me into St James' Park with his shotgun, and took pot-shots at the pelicans and the Ruddy Ducks. He never hit anything, I'm happy to say, but I pointed a lot as if he had, and he would return to Downing Street quite cheered. This did remind me though that as a cat I am meant to be the natural enemy of birds. I only mention this because of what happened later under Mr Major.

Sir Alec was the first of my Prime Ministers to leave Downing Street by the normal method of losing an election. The others had been old or ill. He went back to being Lord Home again, and I think he probably felt more like his old self.

Said Home, 'There are four here, they squeak as I speak.
I'm not counting the twelve in the pelican's beak.'

The man who beat him by four votes was Harold Wilson. Of all the PMs the Harolds were the best in my view. The moment this Harold entered Number Ten, we all moved, lock, stock and barrel into the kitchen, and there we conducted Affairs of State.

These were the Best Years of a Cat's Life. If Trades Union leaders weren't being invited round for beer and sandwiches and a chin-wag, there was a glittering Show-biz party with half the cast of *Coronation Street* dancing the night away. I put on pounds. The carpets were packed with calories. I could never understand how they did it, as they never seemed to have any money.

Harold had a go at joining the Common Market. 'I cannot see', he said over a cup of tea, 'how General de Gaulle can say "No".' General de Gaulle said 'NON!!'. 'I hadn't thought of that,' said Harold, helping himself to a spoonful of my Delikat. Then he devalued the Pound. 'This', he said, 'does not mean the Pound in your pocket has been devalued.' You couldn't help liking the old rogue. Well, some didn't and he lost an election to Edward Heath. But four years later he was back. This time by three votes and still puffing away on his pipe. In public that was. The moment he was back in Number Ten, it was out with the jukebox and Party Time!

You'd never have guessed from all this just how grim things were, with talk of Military Coups, the International Monetary Fund cancelling our overdraft, and the KGB under the kitchen table at Number Ten. It was all very confusing, certainly for a cat.

Suddenly, Harold stood up at breakfast and said, 'I think I'll resign today,' and he did, and it was never that much fun in the kitchen again.

'Let's boogy!' cried Harold, 'let's bop to the beat.
And cat, throw those seven mice into the street.'

Not that the four years of Edward Heath didn't have their moments. You probably see him today as a huge, bad-tempered old fellow with white hair and a red face -

('And a dreadful line in pale blue suits,' adds Old Ginger.)

I remember him rather differently. When Harold's jukebox was taken away by the Removalists, and Edward's Bechstein Grandiosa was installed, my first thought was, 'Will there be no more cakes and ale?' In fact, there weren't. But there *was* the sea, and the music, and Europe. Most of all I remember his wonderful laugh. It began as a low rumble like lemmings tap-dancing, then these frivolous creatures were joined by troupes of clog-dancing bears, his shoulders would rise like the Mighty Wurlitzer from the pit of the Odeon, Leicester Square, and then a great Krakatoa of sound would erupt, registering a least eight point five on the Richter Scale.

There were evenings when he would slip into his silver lamé sailor suit, light the candelabra on the piano and play and sing 'The Best of the Eurovision Song Contest' until tears coursed down his salt-caked cheeks. As I said, he loved the sea, never happier than when at the wheel of *Morning Cloud*, shouting the odds on New Zealand butter into a Force Nine gale. They were exciting times, even if occasionally one felt a little queasy. What a pity that the miners could not share his vision of Great Things to Come. Suddenly, we had the Three-Day Week, and very enjoyable it was. Indeed had he gone into the next election against Harold Wilson, bellowing the joys of the Four-Day Weekend, he might have won. But he didn't, and I must admit I felt a *frisson* of pleasure when I saw the old jukebox being carried into the kitchen.

'Six mice, cat,' said Captain Heath, 'now kindly catch them quick!'
'Oh, come on, mate!' I feebly hail, 'can't you see I'm very sick?'

I almost burst into tears when his successor, Jim Callaghan, strode in. It was the first real whiff of the countryside I'd had since I came to London. He reminded me of all those ruddy-faced farmers who'd come up to Snoring-Snoring Hall to beg Lord Snoring-Snoring not to seize their farms and chattels and sell their wives and daughters into slavery. He wore tweeds and corduroys and Wellington boots. He would never start a Cabinet meeting without a fresh length of straw in his mouth. His ministers never got used to Baldwin the Pig. He'd snuffle about under the Cabinet Room table investigating their red boxes and trouser-legs. As for the chickens, well, cats and chickens have an arrangement, and very rarely bother each other.

All was going well until the Winter of Discontent. I may have mentioned before that humans are very peculiar.

('Indeed you have,' yawns Old Ginger.

'Well, they are!' I cry, 'after all, if cats and chickens can come to an arrangement, why can't humans and humans?')

The dustmen stopped working. All the gravediggers stopped working. I refused to leave the premises. It was very unpleasant out. Chaos. Certainly Unfit for Cats.

In a way, you had to admire old Jim. In the middle of all this, like Lord Nelson before him, Jim said, 'I see no chaos'. Admittedly, when he said it he was on his way back from a Summit Conference in sunny Guadeloupe. He then lost a vote of 'no confidence' in the House of Commons by one vote, the one vote being a mad Scots Nat, thus ushering in One Hundred Years of Mrs Thatcher.

I may have mentioned before that humans are very peculiar.

'They're all on strike,' said Honest Jim, 'except ten blasted mice.
Get rid of them, cat!' 'I'm Going Slow,' I said, 'but name your price.'

When I first saw Mrs Thatcher she was a nice, dumpy little woman standing out in Downing Street, quoting St Francis of Assisi. It sounded like good news for cats:

'Where there is discord, may we bring harmony;
Where there is despair, may we bring hope.'

These thoughts were soon to be shredded. In fact, I think another woman substituted for the first one. The new one was taller, had different teeth and a voice that could make strong men quiver.

I knew this Mrs Thatcher at once. She was exactly like my mother. That look in her eye. That curl in her lip. She could take the face off a Rotweiler with one back-hand swipe, and still be smiling graciously. Just like Mother, Mrs Thatcher treated everyone to the same mixture of lofty disdain and sheer terror, be they old, sick, Argentinean, Neil Kinnock or unemployed.

I used to sit on her husband, Denis. Unlike Sir Winston's heady aroma of brandy and cigars, Denis exuded gin and cigarettes. Apart from those moments when he held me up to protect his head as ashtrays flew, he was comfortable enough. Sometimes, in the early years, Mrs Thatcher would pause in the middle of a tirade and take my milk away. This seemed to calm her. Soon, however, she gave that up and seemed to live in a world of her own. I could see the end coming. Those near to her, whose advice she totally ignored, would slink off into corners and mutter. But I felt almost sorry for her when she went. Even so, to this day when I am abruptly woken from a nap by a limo back-firing in the street or Concorde flying low, my first thought is 'She's back!' and I shudder uncontrollably.

'There are no mice here,' says Mrs T. 'The creatures wouldn't dare!'
'That's odd,' I thought, for I can see a couple over there.'

I should have left when she did, but everything seemed so peaceful by comparison when the Majors moved in, that I was lulled into a false sense of security. There we were cruising along, thinking life was grand, when there was a sudden lurch and we were off the tracks, up the creek and gone, gone, gone. The Low Point was when, amidst all the Sleaze and the Euro-garbage, I was dragged into the columns of the Gutter Press.

Under headlines like 'NUMBER TEN CRISIS OVER AS HUMPHREY THE MOUSER RETURNS TO THE FOLD' I was accused of:
1) being a 'six-year-old tomcat', ('*Six!*' I had high hopes that Old Ginger might explode.) 2) of killing two baby robins – 'favourites of Mr Major', 3) being spotted 'by St James' Park keepers with a duckling in his mouth and 4) being 'officially cleared'.

Are there no depths to which the British Press will not sink in their search for Low Points? In their pursuit of a murky 'scoop'? In their harassment of the innocent?

('Well?' says Old Ginger, 'how innocent are we?')

'One, I'm not six and secondly I deeply resent being "officially cleared" when I was engaged in a cat's proper business. Oh, they're pleased as Punch when you bring them a dead mouse, but you arrive home with the remnants of a dead bird and it's "Naughty Puss! No Whiskas for you tonight." We don't want Whiskas or Kit-E-Kat or Sheba – nine out of ten cats prefer Raw Bird, with Added Rat or Goldfish and Mouse Pie!'

'I think,' said Old Ginger, 'that you speak for us all.')

So I'm off. After all, I only came to look at a Queen and I did that years ago. It's a funny thing, but *she's* not the same woman I met all those years ago.

'I can see it all,' said Major, 'and it looks very nice.
"John Major" they will say, "Oh, yes, and His Four Performing Mice".'

Then, no sooner am I round at Old Ginger's place dictating my Life, than it's 'DOWNING STREET IN MOURNING, Cabinet Office accept that Humphrey went away to die'.

Ha! A pathetic attempt by Major to gain public sympathy and get the animal vote by blubbing over a dead cat and rubbing linseed oil on his Sunburnt Goldfish. How low can they stoop?

I was having none of that and returned at once to Number Ten. Of course, they made a meal of it, with press conferences and photo calls. At the same time, nowadays nothing is too good for me. I click my paw and a man called Gummer attends to my every whim. One day I shall ask for sunburnt goldfish.

('How lucky we are', says Old Ginger, 'that the cat is not a political animal.'

'Unlike', I reply, 'the weasel, the laughing hyena and the sheep.')